W9-AHZ-784

DATE DUE

NO 1 0 08			
MR 1 1 10			
OC 2 7 12			
FE 1 8			
12-08-14			
DE 2 8 14			

Demco, Inc. 38-293

Animals After Dark

BATS

HUNTERS OF THE NIGHT

Elaine Landau

WORDS TO KNOW

colonies—Groups of animals that live together.

echolocation—The process through which bats use sound to identify objects at night.

fertilizer—A substance that makes soil better for growing plants.

fossil—The remains of a plant or animal from millions of years ago

grooming—The way an animal cleans itself.

guano—Bat droppings.

mammal—A an animal that has a warm body temperature. Mammal babies feed on their mothers' milk.

nectar—A sweet fluid produced by flowers.

pollen—Tiny grains from flowering plants that are needed for these plants to reproduce, or make new plants.

rain forest—A thick forest where it rains a lot.

wingspan—The distance between the outer tips of a bat's wings.

CONTENTS

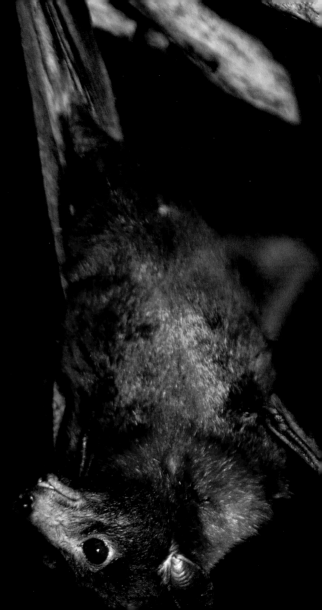

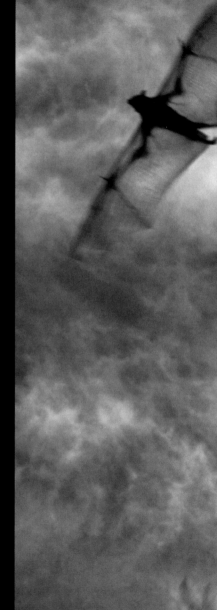

PICTURE THIS . . .

You are camping on a hot summer night. Suddenly, a bat flies in through the tent.

You scream for help. You are sure that the bat wants to bite you. Or maybe it wants to nest in your hair.

Yet, the bat only wants to catch and eat an insect it was chasing. And then, just as suddenly, the bat is gone. It has flown back outside leaving you unharmed. Are you still afraid of bats? You should not be—read on to find out why.

Flying fox bats
begin to hunt
at sunset.

INTRODUCING THE BAT

Humans should not fear bats. They are shy, gentle animals. There are more than one thousand types of bats.

Bats are divided into two main groups. Mega bats are medium- to large-sized bats. Most have long doglike snouts, large eyes, and small ears. They mostly live in tropical places in Australia, Africa, and Asia. These tropical places are hot and have a lot of rain. There are more than 180 different kinds of mega bats.

Flying foxes are the largest mega bats. Their faces look like a fox's—that explains their name. The Malayan flying fox is the world's largest bat. Its body is about the size of a newborn kitten. But with its wings spread, this bat looks huge. It has a wingspan of about six feet. That is about the length of a tall man lying down.

This flying fox bat in Australia has a snout like a dog's and a face like a fox's.

Micro bats are the other group of bats. Most of these bats are smaller than mega bats. Their faces look different too. There are more kinds of micro bats than mega bats. Micro bats can be found throughout much of the world. Forty-seven types of micro bats live in the United States.

The world's smallest micro bat is the hog-nosed bat from Thailand. It is also known as the bumblebee bat because it is the size of a bumblebee. An adult bumblebee bat weighs around two grams, about the weight of a dime. It has a wingspan of under six inches. That is shorter than a pencil.

Look how small the
bumblebee bat is!

ALL ABOUT BATS

Bats are the world's only flying mammals. Mammals are animals with hair that do not usually lay eggs. Almost all mammals give birth to live babies. The German word for bat is *Fledermause* (flay-der-maus). It means "flying mice."

Bats have been around for a long time. Scientists have found bat fossils, or remains, in Wyoming. These date back 55 million years. Bat fossils have also been found in other places in America and the rest of the world.

The earliest bats looked a lot like bats today. But scientists think that they could not fly. Instead, they may have glided through the air.

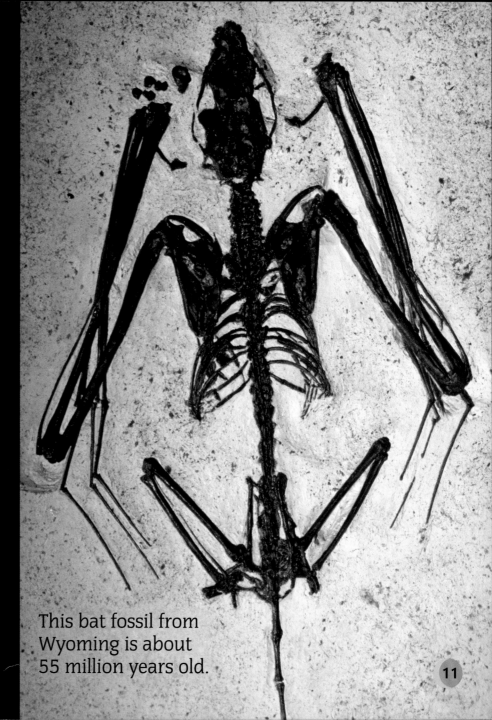

Today, bats are found nearly everywhere. However, these furry fliers do not live in Antarctica or the Arctic. Bats are also not found in the world's hottest deserts.

In China and Japan, bats are thought to bring good luck. The Chinese word for bat is *fu*. It means "good fortune."

This bat fossil from Wyoming is about 55 million years old.

A leaf-nosed bat opens its mouth to make sounds to find prey.

NIGHT LIFE

Bats spend much of the day sleeping and grooming themselves. They do this while hanging upside down. When they are ready to fly, they take off from that position, too.

Most bats begin their flights after dark. These animals are night hunters. They have excellent hearing.

While flying at night, some bats make high-pitched sounds. These sounds create echoes. The echoes let the bat know where different objects are. The echoes take the place of seeing the object.

This is called echolocation (eh-koh-loh-kay-shun). It helps bats find and catch insects to eat. It even lets the bat know how large an insect is without seeing it.

FEEDING TIME!

Though many bats eat insects, not all bats are meat eaters. Many mega bats eat fruits like mangoes and bananas. Others use their long snouts to lap up nectar from flowers.

Some micro bats also eat fruit, but most eat insects. They eat flies, mosquitoes, beetles, spiders, and cockroaches. One brown bat can eat about six hundred insects in an hour.

A few kinds of bats eat fish, frogs, scorpions, small birds, lizards, and rats.

This bat has caught a nice, juicy insect!

Only three types of bats drink blood. These vampire bats live in Central and South America.

One type of vampire bat bites a cow, horse, mule, or pig to get blood. Vampire bats may seem scary, but they are not very large.

THE BAT CAVE AND MORE

Do you think that all bats live in caves? Some do, but others can be found in old mines, trees, bridges, tunnels, and cracks in rock. They live in forests, fields, and near lakes, ponds, and streams. Bats are even found in cities.

Many bats live together in colonies. A large colony can have millions of bats. The world's largest bat colony is in Bracken Cave in Texas. During the summers, as many as 20 million Mexican free-tailed bats may roost there.

Other bats live by themselves. Many more live in pairs.

In the winter, some bats migrate, or travel, to warmer places. Others hibernate, spending the winter in a deep sleep. This helps them to live through the winter when there is little food.

A vampire-bat colony on a tree trunk.

A ghost bat comes out of hiding at night to hunt.

STAYING ALIVE

There are few animals that eat bats in the wild. However, at times, hawks, snakes, cats, and weasels eat them. Yet bats are often able to avoid these animals. During the day, they roost, or sit and rest, in high or hidden places where many animals cannot get to them.

As a result, bats live longer than many mammals their size. Some types of bats live for more than

MATING AND RAISING YOUNG

Some types of male bats sing to attract the females for mating. After mating, the female bat will have babies.

Bat babies are called pups. Usually bats have one pup at a time. Yet some types of bats may have two or even four pups. Like all mammals, mother bats nurse, or feed their pups milk. Mother bats can always find their pups out of thousands in a roost. They know their pups by their cry and how they smell.

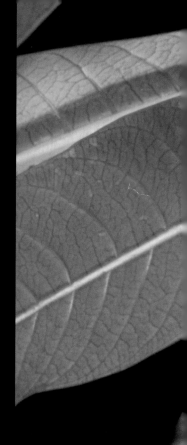

A Gambian bat mother holds its pup tight as they both hang upside down.

This bat is eating fruit from the Saguaro cactus plant.

HOW BATS HELP

Bats are helpful to humans. Micro bats eat harmful insects. Many of these insects destroy crops and spread disease.

Bats that drink nectar are important, too. As these bats sip a flower's nectar, pollen collects on their fur. When they fly to other flowers, they spread the pollen. This lets new plants grow.

Fruit-eating bats are needed as well. These bats drop fruit seeds as they eat. The seeds grow into new plants.

Bat droppings, called guano (gwa-no), also contain seeds that grow. Bat guano is useful to farmers, too. It is an excellent fertilizer for their crops.

THE FUTURE

Many bats are disappearing. In some places, bats have lost their homes. This is especially true in tropical rain forests.

Often these areas have been cleared to make way for farms, houses, and towns. When this happens, the bats there often die. People remain the biggest threat to bats today. Seventy-five types of bats are at risk of dying out. Those in the United States include the gray bat, the Indiana bat, and the Ozark big-eared bat.

A person holds
an Indiana bat.

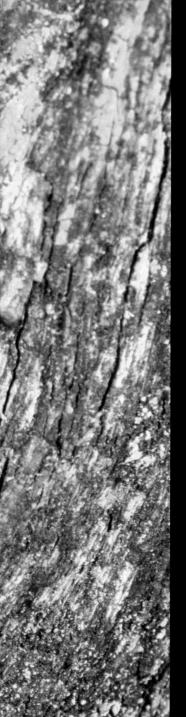

Laws in some areas protect bats. However, these laws are not always obeyed. Some people have come together to protect bats. They protect the places where bats roost.

They also have urged people to build bat houses in their yards. This would let bats safely roost. There are even bat rescue centers for injured bats.

Many bats make forests their homes. When trees get cut down, it is hard for these bats to find a new home.

Vampire bats feed on the blood of other animals.

FUN FACTS ABOUT BATS

⭐ Bat guano is rich in nitrogen (ny-tra-jen)—a colorless, odorless gas. That makes it a good fertilizer for farming.

⭐ Have you ever heard the saying, "Blind as a bat?" Bats are not blind. Some have very good eyesight.

⭐ A bat can find an insect up to eighteen feet away using echolocation.

⭐ Bats can carry rabies. Rabies is a disease that can be passed from bats and other mammals to people. If someone with rabies is not treated quickly, that person will die. Very few bats ever get rabies.

⭐ Vampire bats are the only mammals that live entirely on blood.

⭐ Some types of bats will bring food to an ill bat that cannot hunt. Female bats have also cared for bat babies whose mothers have died.

TO KNOW MORE ABOUT BATS

BOOKS

Dornfeld, Margaret. *Bats.* Tarrytown, N.Y.: Benchmark Books, 2005.

Mason, Adrienne. *Bats.* Tonawanda, N.Y.: Kids Can Press, 2003.

Riley, Joelle. *Bats.* Minneapolis, Minn.: Lerner Books, 2005.

Welsbacher, Anne. *Vampire Bats.* Mankato, Minn.: Capstone, 2001.

INTERNET ADDRESSES

Bat Conservation International

Visit this Web site to learn how to help bats. The KidZ Cave link has fun bat games, puzzles, and arts and crafts.

<http://www.batcon.org>

Connecticut Department of Environmental Protection— Batty About Bats Web site.

This great Web site for kids has lots of cool facts about bats.

<http://www.ct.gov/dep/cwp/ view.asp?a=2723&q= 326178&depNav_GID=1655>

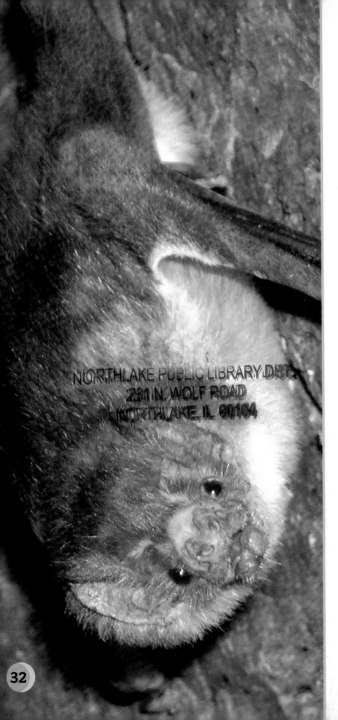

Enslow Elementary, an imprint of Enslow Publishers, Inc.

Enslow Elementary® is a registered trademark of Enslow Publishers, Inc.

Library of Congress Cataloging-in-Publication Data

Landau, Elaine.
    Bats : hunters of the night / Elaine Landau.
        p. cm. — (Animals after dark)
    Includes bibliographical references and index.
    ISBN-13: 978-0-7660-2772-5
    ISBN-10: 0-7660-2772-4
    1. Bats—Juvenile literature. I. Title. II. Series.
QL737.C5L2 2007
599.4—dc22   2006014967

Printed in the United States of America

10 9 8 7 6 5 4 3 2

To Our Readers: We have done our best to make sure all Internet Addresses in this bo were active and appropriate when we went to press. However, the author and the publis er have no control over and assume no liability for the material available on those Interr sites or on other Web sites they may link to. Any comments or suggestions can be sent e-mail to comments@enslow.com or to the address on the back cover.

Series Literacy Advisor: Dr. Allan A. De Fina, Department of Literacy Education, N Jersey City University.

Illustration Credits: B. G. Thomson/Photo Researchers, Inc., pp. 6–7, 18–19; Carst Peter/National Geographic/Getty Images, p. 17; © Hugo Willoc/Foto Natura/Mind Pictures, pp. 26–27; Indiana DNR/Rich Fields, pp. 24–25; © Joe McDonald/Visua Unlimited, pp. 1; © 2006 Jupiterimages, p. 2; © Ken Lucas/Visuals Unlimited, p. 11; I Merlin D. Tuttle/Bat Conservation International/PhotoResearchers, Inc., pp. 8–9, 14– 20–21, 22–23; © Michael & Patricia Fogden/Minden Pictures, p. 28; Paul A. Zahl/Natior Geographic/Getty Images, pp. 12–13; © Regis Martin/Lonely Planet Images, pp. 4– Shutterstock, pp. 3, 29, 32.

Cover Illustration: © Joe McDonald/Visuals Unlimited (front and back cover).

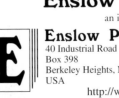

Enslow Elementary
an imprint of
Enslow Publishers, Inc.
40 Industrial Road
Box 398
Berkeley Heights, NJ 07922
USA
http://www.enslow.com